Quantum

Chungliang Al Huang

Soup

Fortune Cookies in Crisis

CELESTIALARTS

Berkeley, California

CELESTIAL ARTS
P.O. Box 7327
Berkeley, California 94707

First draft editor: Denise McCluggage
Editor: Suzanne Pierce
Cover design by Ken Scott
Text design and production by David Charlsen
Typesetting by Recorder Typesetting Network

ISBN: 0-89087-504-9
Library of Congress Catalog Card Number: 90-81457

0 9 8 7 6 5 4 3 2 1
95 94 93 92 91

Manufactured in Singapore

Quantum Soup

A Note on Romanization

None of the existing romanized systems is fully satisfactory to render the correct pronunciation of Chinese. I am adopting the new Chinese spelling called pin-yin (literal meaning: combined sounds) for the usual spelling: T'ai Chi, now Tai Ji, looks more like the way it sounds. I have left many words as they have been written by most standard systems of romanization. By now most readers are familiar with Tao, which is actually pronounced Dow. I Ching is pronounced E Jing, and Tan-t'ien is Dantien. And the eight trigrams: Ch'ien, K'un, K'an, Li, Sun, Ch'en, T'ui and Ken should be pronounced close to Chi-en, Koo-en Ka-an, Lee-i, Sue-en, Tzen, Dui and Gen.

Why Quantum Soup?

Imagine going to a Chinatown Sunday Dim Sum (tea brunch) with a roundtable of stimulating friends to discuss the meaning of life and to join in the sampling of successes, failures, tears, and laughter ... from the most mystical to the most obvious, from profundity to cornball, from Quantum Soup to Fortune Cookies.

Quantum Soup suggests a light and delightful broth with philosophical noodles. *Dim Sum* literally means "a touch of heart," delicacies to be served in small portions, freshly flavored and steaming hot, brought to you continually on a food cart to entice you. You are free to choose those items that sing out to you for your enjoyment and effortless digestion.

Quantum is a popular word these days, but few know its meaning. *Won*, meaning "cloud"; and *Ton* meaning "to swallow." Poetically, wonton is a tasty morsel to be swallowed lightly, like a puff of cloud! Like Wonton soup in Chinese dinners, many people like it, but few bother to find out what's in it.

If we delve into the lingo of new physics, quantum is that elusive, cloudlike mystery of "nonbeing" essence, which is best swallowed lightly in spite of its complexity. And, as with all Chinese food, you are hungry for more a few minutes later.

I delight in fortune cookies! I find them one of the most ingenious of indigenous American inventions. Do you realize that there is no such thing as a fortune cookie in China, nor such standbys as Chop Suey and Egg Foo Yung? I relish this kind of creative flexibility and casual adaptation.

Before I set foot on the American shore, my notion of Americans was sharply divided between two stereotypes: the 1950s "Ugly Americans" and the singing-and-dancing Ginger Rogers and Fred Astaires. I think we all have the tendency to generalize according to our own limited experiences. Admit it! Until recently, didn't you visualize the Chinese as Pearl S. Buck's *Good Earth* characters or the buck-toothed, almond-eyed laundrymen, waiters, Fu Manchus, and Charlie Chans?

My first exposure to America was as a freshman in a small college town. I discovered and became addicted to a local "gleasy flied lice" hangout called Chinese Tea Room. It was there I fell in love with the fortune cookies! I was impressed by how those mythical sage-writers could turn out such an endless supply of such often apt and succinct sayings. Both the cookies and the wisdom were always easily digestible, practical, universal, and so . . . accessible!

Later, when I became a post-graduate intellectual snob, I belittled the "everything in the kitchen sink" (actual

In Crisis

meaning for Chop Suey) representation of Chinese food; and was gratified to see an introduction of the more sophisticated Mandarin, Szechuan, and Hunan cuisines. Always, however, the fortune cookies remained and flourished. Where else could one find such instant wisdom as "The only certainty is the uncertainty of the certainty" and "He who trips over the same stone twice deserves to break neck!" or " You are much too intelligent to be carried away by flattery," and, perhaps, "Paradox is ego standing on its head attracting attention!"

Crisis is a big word these days. Everybody and everything is in crisis. What does it mean? My fortune cookie tells me to look into its origin in Chinese written language: The two characters are *Wei* (危) and *Chi* (機). *Wei* ("danger") shows a face-to-face encounter with a powerful animal like a tiger; *Chi* ("opportunity") is the blueprint or scheme of the universe. Therefore, crisis is both danger and opportunity! In crisis, if we don't panic and despair but learn to reach within for the spontaneity of our wisdom, we will be ready to take full advantage of the new opportunities opening to us.

Crisis promotes the learning of polarity—the interweavings of seeming opposites in delicate balance: love/hate, gain/loss, success/failure, man/woman, light/dark, war/peace . . . the entire spectrum of the yin/yang dance!

Are the fortune cookies in crisis?

Old-fashioned direct wisdom appears out of vogue nowadays. We strive for pseudoinscrutability to escape having to receive the core message. Much of our intellectual outpouring is junk and pollution. It is threatening to overrun our minds and hearts! It's even slithering into my highly esteemed fortune cookies. Junk thoughts are taking over the fortune cookie factory! I can see it now—an assembly line for the new age mystics, blissfully stuffing profundities in each cookie's "lotus"!

This book is a spring housecleaning for the mind and body. *Quantum Soup* is like great-grandma's panacea, good for whatever ails you! "Drink it . . . you'll like it!"

The recipes herein are the amalgamation of my EastWest heritage, to be practiced and lived for joyful cultivation of the philosophical gourmet, to better serve you with Dim Sum goodies.

With respect and a "a touch of heart," I offer you a light and de-light-ening feast of the mindbody. Take your time with the "cloud-swallowing" Quantum Menu. Enjoy!

Crisis

扰 ß 毛

Danger

and

Opportunity

笑

Laughing

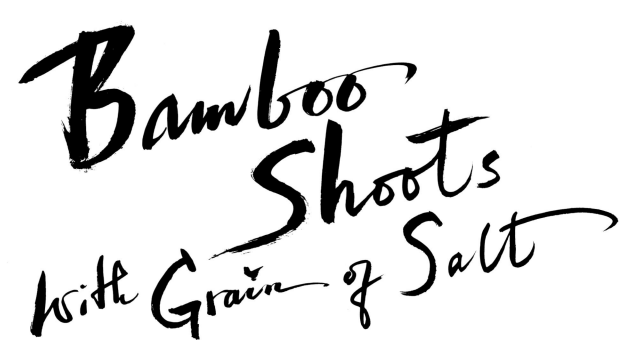

Bamboo Shoots with Grain of Salt

Laughter in Chinese writing is depicted by a human with arms and legs flung wide apart, head up to the sky, vibrating with mirth like bamboo leaves in the wind.

Listen! The sound of true laughter is as open and clear as the flute-heart of bamboo. We are like that. Breathe through us freely and we make heavenly music.

But so few of us laugh like that. Saying "cheese" for a photograph or a tee-hee behind a hand is not a full quaking-bamboo-leaf laugh. It does not resonate through the body fully, clearing the congestion in all the channels.

To grow a proper laugh, start with the image of a baby shoot pushing up through the earth. Start with just the thoughts of laughter. Don't hurry it. Let it grow like the shoot. Wait for a genuine smile. Let it widen as a sound begins to tickle in the throat. Now let it begin to bounce around in the chest. Still, do not hurry it!

Think now of the rapidly growing bamboo, rising to the sun, leaves atremble in the fresh spring air. Allow your body to follow the leaves, expanding in all directions. Your breath is bigger, deeper, wider. *S-t-r-e-t-c-h-i-n-g*. Let it grow. Watch it go. *Now* give it its sound!

A chuckle shakes the shoulders; a guffaw is born in the belly. *Haw—haw—haw—haw*! How it escapes through the mouth and quakes and shakes and blooms and booms. Your very fingers are atingle with it. Your toes and kneecaps and hips and lips become the very sound of laughter. It is everywhere. *Haw-haw-haw*! ("Is that *me*?" you think, and laugh ever more fully and freely at the absurdity of the thought.)

Bam-bam-bam-boo . . . bamboozling you.

Haw—haw—haw!

13

One of the most highly recommended Taoist and Zen meditations is to let your hair down, stick out your belly and roar with laughter. Shall we fantasize this ritual for all the great world leaders? Laughter can be particularly purifying for them during one of those important summit meetings where they gather to decide the fate of our world.

The very same *Haw-haw-haw* quaking and shaking can also be a good and healthy cry.

In the Chinese writing, the same human character, with brush strokes looking like arms and legs flung wide apart, is allowing tears to gush from the openings of the eyes and all emotional and energy channels.

Why do we hide tears and insist on restraining our natural expressions of feeling?

When was the last time you experienced a hearty, releasing cry?

Tears can be a most effective cleansing ritual as well. During funerals in China, we hire professional criers to help us continue the drama of all necessary expressions of grief. We yell and scream our regrets and guilts with great gusto. By the time we have cried our eyes dry and our hearts out, we are released and at peace.

So . . .

Cry a lot.

Laugh a lot.

Enjoy being the great and healthy human.

crying

Buddha on Draft

In the Christian world, those who think they are Jesus Christ or God are usually confined behind walls and given therapy. They would be better off—or at least freer to roam—if they claimed to be Buddha. Buddha is not something separate to be worshipped as a supreme being. *Buddha* literally means "the awakened one," and being Buddha—or more accurately *a* Buddha—is within the aspirations of anyone.

Nor is Buddha revered in the same way as Western saints or holy ones are. Zen followers are encouraged to *kill* the Buddha. It is not, strictly speaking, murder but rather a part of a cycle. We meet Buddha, kill him, and thus make way for the awakening of another Buddha as often as possible. This is how we progress in the understanding of our own Buddhahood. (Just don't get Buddha confused with Christ.)

Ancient legend tells about the birth of Buddha:
" . . . *from the sky two pure streams of water fell, refreshing the child and its mother, after which the infant, standing upright, facing East, strode forward seven steps, pointed upward with his right hand, downward with his left, and shouted with a noble voice the victory shout of all the Buddhas:*
'Worlds above, worlds below! The chief in all the worlds am I!'"

—JOSEPH CAMPBELL, *The Mythic Image*

17

Here's an exercise to help awaken the Buddha in you. Stand firmly but not tensely, with your feet easily wide apart. Let your arms open roundly to the sky, face upward, chest high but easy. Breathe fully but without force. Now imagine two pure streams of water pouring from the heavens and washing over you.

Splash in the water with your arms flailing.

Open your mouth to the cooling downpour.

Let yourself fill with the joy and power of this gift.

When you are thoroughly refreshed, take seven strides to the east, point upward with your right hand, downward with your left and announce:

"Worlds above, worlds below!
The chief in all the worlds am I!"

Can you keep from laughing at this arrogance! Oh, I hope not. Because the laugh is what really awakens you.

Wake up!

18

Take the "S" out of Cosmic

The benefit and wisdom of laughter is now crystal clear. And why do so many of us insist on cheerless sobriety? Out third eye is shut tight or turned inward with a frown.

Turn the eye around and take a good look at some of our cosmic jokes.

Take the *s* out of the cosmic and enjoy what's left. If you honestly understand a joke and if you can laugh at it and fall in it, you've got the joke. You are the joke! Exercise the joke on you. Let your third eye wink back. You'll trip and fall and bounce right back, light and brighter, laughing all the way home!

Don't limit your vision only to yourself; benefit others with your good humor. Do you have an unbearable person in your life's circle? Fantasize and let your eye capture that person getting a flouride treatment in the dentist's chair. Cap on those bulging, oozing, sour gums over the person's teeth. Then wedge in a chilling suction tube between. Listen to its embarassing juicy gurgle. Stand back and take a good look at your handiwork.

Can you laugh at him now, sitting there helpless and ridiculous? That person *is* you, too!

How Chinese is this fable!

The ancient story has it that heaven and hell are exactly alike in that each is an enormous banquet with every wonderful dish imaginable crowding the great round table. The diners are provided with chopsticks—five feet long!

In hell, the diners give up struggling to feed themselves with these impossible tools and sit in ravenous frustration.

In heaven, everyone simply feeds the person across the table.

How to use Chopsticks properly

Roast Faux Pas or Grace at the Table

I think of three stories, American and Chinese.

At thanksgiving dinner the assembled family and guests all have eyes on the maid as she carries in the platter with an enormous, perfectly browned turkey. Their expressions turn to horror as she trips and falls and sends the bird skittering across the floor. The hostess collects herself and says calmly: "Marie, if you are unhurt, pick up that turkey, take it to the kitchen, and *bring in the other one*."

At a stodgy and ostentatious fund-raising dinner, a well-meaning American lady tried to be hospitable to the Chinese gentleman sitting next to her. She asked him, enunciating carefully, "Likey soupee?" He smiled. And later, "Likey chickee?" He nodded. Then the man was announced as the keynote speaker of the gala event.

After much applause, he returned to his seat and turned to the woman: "Likey speechee?"

The late Chou En-lai was host at a banquet for visiting historian, Theodore White. As a roast suckling pig was ceremoniously presented to honor White, Chou suddenly realized that White was Jewish. He salvaged the frozen moment by indicating the porcine dish and saying: "Come Ted, let's try some of the Peking duck." And they did.

Loontil Soup avec Schmaltz

Sometimes, as a background to my Tai Ji,* I like some lush, romantic music—Viennese waltzes, syrupy strings—I call it "Tai Ji Schmaltz" and find it good for the soul, and for the souls in my classes. A current favorite is the soundtrack from an Academy Award-winning Hollywood movie, richly sentimental right down to the laughing of the loons.†

When the loons laugh on the record, who can keep from joining them? What was getting heavy lightens immediately, and we call out puns to one another—with the corn as high as an elephant's eye.

"I vant to be a-loon," "A-loon at last."

Croon me a looney tune. Come fry with me. Tao Be Do Be Tao!

I find in the West many people "do" Tai Ji or "practice" it—rather ponderous words, perhaps accounting for the serious demeanor of many Tai-Ji–doing faces. But the true translation from the Chinese Da–"beat," "the beat" or "hit it, man!"—is to play and enjoy Tai Ji.

What fun it is to play Tai Ji, sharing smiles and laughs and loons with others. Why must we assume that getting in tune with the universe means silence and solemnity, aching leg poses, and dour expressions? Perhaps that is one way, but it is not my way.

---

*The new pin-yin Chinese spelling for T'ai Chi.
†Do you realize that the loons have had 160,000,000 years of laughing practice?

I admit that some conscientious searchers for the path are often put off by my lighthearted approach and Midwestern, corny humor. They say that I do not do "real" Tai Ji, I only dance it! Once, when I taught a group in Germany, a woman tearfully told me that she could do nothing else but go out and kill herself because I had made fun of everything she held in reverence. (I later learned she periodically threatened such action.) I tried to explain to her that finding fun in everything is not the same as making fun of it.

When I read G. K. Chesterton's line: "Angels fly because they take themselves lightly," I was de*light*ed. At the same time, I was saddened that this world is still so short of heaven.

Not that all must be levity and lighter-than-air. We can take our cue for a Tai Ji balance from the Chinese characters for *tree*, a well-rooted object, and *flight*, airborne. Notice how the downward brush strokes in *Mu* ("tree" 木) are balanced by the outward reaching ones? And the flight of the bird is pictured here, *Fei* (飛), with a pair of wings (飞飞) flapping upward (升).

I see these brush lines as not *doing* tree or bird but *dancing* them in the true spirit of the Tai Ji Loon-iverse. If you find no such dance in your philosophies and deep wisdom, let loose the loon and laugh.

"I call no man wise until he has made the progress from the wisdom of knowledge to the wisdom of foolishness, and become a laughing philosopher . . . "

—LIN YUTANG, *The Importance of Living*

Riding on the Wind

Chopstick Your Piano

I know someone with a beautiful Steinway grand, but she never plays it anymore. She says that she can't bear to hear herself after attending an Arthur Rubinstein concert.

I doubt that it is the intention of the masters to intimidate their listeners into silence. I think it is more likely that they would like to inspire their audience into greater enjoyment of their own playing. Yet too many people allow their self-judgments to paralyze their activities.

Many persons come to my Tai Ji seminars and workshops apologizing for their awkwardness. I congratulate them. At least they are there—aware. They are interested in becoming more acquainted with their bodies. How many other people treat their bodies as if they were rented from Hertz—something they are using to get around in but nothing they genuinely care about understanding? Recognizing awkwardness is already a long way toward not being awkward anymore.

Besides, what is awkward?

I start out with new students by getting them to recognize that *awkward* is really just a word for their own notions about what *other* people are thinking of them. But that is an *assumption,* a guess, a belief born of self-consciousness. When we are worried that other people will find us awkward, that very worry constricts movements and tightens muscles and—lo and behold!—we *are* awkward.

How to break the vicious circle?

I tell people to begin very simply so that it is easier not to get in their own way with their assumptions of judgments. I point out that they do not seem to worry that people will judge harshly the way they sit in a chair or step up a curb. So I suggest they begin by keeping their movements simple, gradually exploring new territory.

25

I tell them to pretend that the others are trees or rocks or flowers or weeds. After all, they do not concern themselves that the pine tree is critical of their dancing or that the pebbles are snickering among themselves over the stiffness of their arm movements. If that person there is a juniper and those are speckled rocks and these a field of daisies—how freeing from judgments that can be! Nature neither condemns nor applauds us. Let people be as nature.

Such freedom can open a body to the discovery of spontaneous grace and improvised beauty. That does not always seem a comfortably secure path for some, and many students prefer the safety of learning strictly prescribed postures—as if following a gridded street map. Though their movements may always be posed and mechanical—and thus miss the essence of Tai Ji—the formality is at least protection against trying to flow and being judged an awkward failure.

A new student at one of my workshops refused to move at all without knowing exactly what to do next. When he couldn't think of what he was "supposed" to do next, he froze! Often, in our free exercises, what he was "supposed" to do was whatever he felt like doing; therefore, he was usually incapable of moving at all.

Day after day he stood and watched the others becoming more and more adventuresome in their explorations. It was obvious that he suffered intensely from his self-imprisonment, and the pressure inside him built.

Then one morning, by the seashore, his body slipped the tight reins of his controlling mind, and he adopted the waves and the birds wheeling overhead as his models. He moved with them, as them, and for several breakthrough moments he was breathtakingly graceful.

Later, a bystander said to him: "Wow, that was beautiful! You must have practiced Tai Ji for a long time."

"Yup!" was the student's proud and spontaneous answer. "All my life!"

"Grandma Always Danced!"

One of the greatest dance mimes, Lotte Goslar, is a divine clown, a performer's performer. She is one of my mentors, a beautiful person I admire and am inspired by. She celebrates dancing from cradle to old age. In her renowned solo "Grandma Always Danced!," we even find her dancing as an angel. Here are a few morsels from her special blend of *Quantum Soup:*

ON COMPASSION

As a child, Lotte decided she must paint pictures on the underside of tables and chairs so her cat and the mice might also have something pretty to look at.

ON ILLUSION

Taking her final curtain call at the end of a concert in Europe, Lotte was thrilled with the nonstop applause from the audience. Lotte came on stage again and again to take a bow. Finally, she became suspicious of the reality of her overwhelming glory. She took a careful look beyond the footlights. It was a standing ovation—for the king and the queen in their royal box. She had been bowing graciously and happily to the *backs* of the audience the entire time!

ON BEAUTY

As an excited young dancer making her debut in Germany, dressed in a confection of ruffles and lace, she was eagerly arranged in her opening pose. As the curtain parted, a voice in the front row muttered, "God, she's ugly!"

Many years later, when she was on the stage of the Jacob's Pillow Dance Festival, the curtain opened to reveal Lotte in the exact same pose. Someone in the front row gasped, "God, she's *beautiful!*"

Dancing Energy

Potted Shrimp

Adults often indulge in a handy ruse—that shade of truth called the white lie. When we don't wish to hurt other people's feelings unnecessarily, we pretend to go along, sincerely insincere, with whatever the occasion calls for, delighting in our glib diplomacy and disguise of ambiguity.

Children have no such ploy. They are blunt, often to the point of pain. They let us know exactly what they think, see, and feel. When my daughters join me in my dance practice, I lose them to snickers and boredom the minute I start self-consciously *dahn*cing my technique.

Adults may come to respect and admire the disciplined production of art, but children are not bound by education and refined opinion. They *naturally* reject the *unnatural* and readily poke fun at it without apology or regret.

The first time Lark (then two and a half) saw a ballet program on TV, she burst out laughing and giggling about the "tippy-toed" fluttering. My other daughter, Tysan, used to beg me to change the dial whenever an affected technique-laden voice began to sing on FM radio.

Now we are chauffeuring our children to seemingly endless dance and music lessons. Gradually, they are learning to appreciate the quality that results from a "defined" movement or a "toned" voice. But they continue to reject technique without spirit and affectation without spontaneity. They are not impressed by quadruple pirouettes or coloratura trills unless the performer evokes in them a genuine sympathetic chord.

Why do some artists, with their superb training, move and sound effortless and pure, whereas others appear strained and affected? Why do some intellectual giants speak and write with eloquent simplicity, whereas others insist on being purposefully evasive and mind-boggling?

Tse Sze, the grandson of Confucius, said: "That which is God-given is called nature; to follow that nature is called Tao; to arrange the Tao is called culture." So often we learned people, in our refinement of nature, forget the Tao—the essence of nature. We cultivate cultivations, developing a distortion ranging far from natural.

In the Western world something called topiary turns trees into fanciful creatures, as stylistically barbered as French poodles and as far from the natural state as possible. And in the Orient the practice of bonsai vividly illustrates the distinction between *nature* and controlled cultivation. Trees many years old have been trained to grow no higher than a kitten. I find a tree with trimmed roots and braced branches, trained to suit a human standard, definitely "unplant"! To me it is akin to the practice of purposely maiming a child so he'll receive more sympathy when set out on the street to beg.

A tree's nature is to grow like a tree, not in some dwarfed version to match a human ideal of a symbolic tree—however charming and impressive the result might be.

How would you like to be cultivated to follow some alien aesthetic?

How would you like to be a bonsai person, a shrimp-sized human in a flowerpot?

On Viewing Flowers

In Ray Bradbury's "Fahrenheit 451," a two-hundred-foot-long billboard was built along the superhighway so that people in fast-moving vehicles could read the entire message.

We can, right now, supersonically span continents and leap oceans—a useful feat—yet many of us are like dragonflies, tap-tapping on water without truly landing anywhere. Have we grown so used to the pace that slowing down is frightening? Are we afraid of what things might look like close-up—no longer blurred by distance or speed? Are we still up in the air even after landing? Parents use a powerful metaphor when their teenagers transgress—they "ground" them as punishment. Are they making them flighty in response?

It seems that we could better match our speed and altitude to the task at hand. Flowers are not ideally viewed from a galloping horse, yet the galloping horse is singularly appropriate for a chukker of polo.

In Tai Ji classes, some beginning students are ponderously earthbound and seek to plant each leg as firmly as a tree trunk when they move. Other beginners barely touch the earth and bounce around like silly putty. Tai Ji helps both—helps one to stretch the viny bonds that hold him down, and helps the other to settle enough to connect with roots. Balance is the outcome.

Flight is appropriate for a bee to get from one flower to another but not for us. If flower viewing is our intent, rein in our galloping steed, dismount, and look.

from a Galloping Horse

Horse

走马看花

Recipe for Recovery

East is East
West is West
And so is jet lag . . . .

No matter how used to traveling I become or how much I enjoy it, I still find it a strain on my physical and mental well-being. I sometimes successfully offset this displacement by consciously applying all my hard-won tricks and disciplines to keep the various parts of my body and mind synchronous with the rapidly passing time zones.

  I practice a restricted Tai Ji in the back of the airplane aisle or an even more subtle version sitting in my cramped center seat! I listen to soothing music on the earphones. I visualize a progression of colors. I meditate on the various symbols of my kundalini circulation. I make my breathing consciously full. And I eat lightly and sensibly.

  At times I have even tucked a small bag of garden earth from home to hold near my center for "grounding." Yet on some trips the drain of jet lag can be stronger than all my craftiness, and I find my biological rhythm clashing with my surroundings for a day or two. There have been two magical transcendences.

I had been invited to teach a special course in Tai Ji for Yehudi Menuhin's music school in England. When I arrived in London, I was totally off-balance; my mini-Tai Ji and bag of garden earth had failed me.

The music of Bach's *Chaconne* received me immediately as I entered Menuhin's house. Yehudi was coaching a young violinist in this monumental marvel. Finishing his instruction, Yehudi continued to play and urged me to join him with Tai Ji dancing.

At home I often dance to Menuhin's recording of *Chaconne*, but in this looking-glass world, I was dancing to Yehudi—live!—in his own music room. Every cell in my body responded to this music. The music and movement were knitting me back into harmony. For a few blissful moments the furnishings and the walls of the room disappeared to be replaced by palpable sound. I was again flying—this time, solidly grounded.

My travel travail was gone!

Another time, I was in Bombay, where I had gone for an international conference. Still completely dis-Oriented after an exhausting flight halfway around the globe, I was implored by the chairman of the event to substitute for the ailing Dalai Lama, who was to have given the keynote address. Not being sufficiently alert to realize the enormity of what I was agreeing to, I let myself be led on stage. There I encountered before me a ballroom-full of anxious faces belonging to similarly dazed people who had traveled similarly long ways.

I sensed that they, like me, longed for a restoration of balance with the world they had traversed. I suggested to them that we invoke whatever forces we usually call up by whatever name—God, Tao, Nature—to guide us in healing the rift between our bodies and our world.

We focused on our inner resources and practiced Tai Ji motifs to open our minds and bodies to the cleansing and healing power of the five elements—fire, water, wood, metal, earth. Within half an hour everyone in the congress seemed miraculously enlivened.

As we began to feel our own vitality and equilibrium return, we visualized the Dalai Lama among us, offering him our healing energies in reciprocation for his benevolence.

These occasions confirmed my belief that the power to readjust our internal clocks is within us, an ability to realign ourselves with the universe in spite of fierce displacements.

Sometimes, as in these two instances, it took the added power of another individual or a group to assist in countering a particularly strong disruption. But ultimately the power is our own.

火

木 田 金

水

Chrysanthemum Shish-Kebob

"Is Tai Ji a martial art?" I am often asked. Since the answer is a complicated one, I often simplify it. "Yes, it is, but a happy martial art."

Some of us, concerned with the excessively yang aspects of the martial arts as taught in America (a friend calls them "the *macho* arts"), organized the Happy Martial Arts Festival in California several years ago. We wanted to balance the impression of aggressive force. The festival poster showed a samurai in his usual sword-slashing posture, but instead of a sword he wielded a giant chrysanthemum.

As a child in China, I was told by a kung fu teacher: "It is easy to meditate quietly gazing at a candle flame. What is not so easy is to meditate on a fist coming at your face—and turn it into a flower."

One of my Tai Ji students was mugged outside a New York subway station. She recalled the exact moment of "off-centeredness" that must have marked her as an easy target. She recovered enough composure to receive the blow with complete resilience—turning it into a flower—and was herself unharmed, even though she lost her purse.

Another Tai Ji friend was set upon outside his hotel in Paris. His attacker aimed a fist at his chin as he tried to snatch his briefcase. My friend automatically absorbed the force of the blow with a spin and ended up facing the attacker in a firm stance; he let out such a collected roar that the would-be thief fled like a wounded pup.

No less astonished than my friend were his teen-aged children, who had previously been embarrassed by their father's practice of "weird," slow-moving Tai Ji. So impressed were they that afterward they insisted on repeat demonstrations every time a new friend visited their home.

Many people study the more martial of martial arts consciously preparing for action, whether in self-defense or in active demonstration of their power. Their sword, however symbolic, is carried openly in their belt. Often it is interpreted by others as a challenge, and often, therefore, they have occasion to use it.

The happy martial artist carries his art as a chrysanthemum, lighter in weight than the steely sword and sweeter of scent. It is unthreatening, and yet sheathed within it is a sword every bit as useful as the one carried openly.

Another Lousy Sunset in Paradise

Whenever possible, I choose inspiring natural surroundings for my Living Tao seminars. The broad skies help to raise our spirits and expand our views. Ocean waves and mountain clouds demonstrate movement in constancy with our bodies. We rejoice in whatever the weather, "singing and dancing in the rain," and we never miss our daily Tai Ji ritual of helping to elevate the sun each dawning and attending to its proper setting each evening.

In normal everyday existence, it is not as easy to refresh ourselves so spontaneously. The workaday routine rarely finds us out welcoming the rising sun, and we let the sun go down any old way it can. We are weary with its regularity and

can be stirred only by the truly spectacular productions, with rich color transforming the clouds. We thus become addicts of the *peak* experiences and devalue the virtues of the ordinary.

Cast a responsive eye at your surroundings, wherever you are. Find the appeal in the commonplace. Admire the past full moon for its very lopsidedness. See the beauty in the faded bloom. Pause while the smog-dulled sun drops from the leaden sky.

Let yourself remember the small wonders of this earth; settle with its subtle turning motion. Don't wait for the technicolor splash of rose and saffron on puffy clouds.

For a moment you may find yourself tuned into the beat of the cosmic dance that goes on even when the colored spotlights are out.

"The circular movement which assures the survival of the same things by repeating them, by bringing about their continuous return, is the perfect and most immediate expression (hence that which is closest to the divine) of the absolute immobility at the summit of hierarchy . . . . Cosmic time is repetition and anakuklosis, eternal return."
—HENRI-CHARLES PUECH, *Man and Time*

"Repeat and reverse . . . you'll realize that you cannot repeat—it'll always be a new experience!"

—JOSEF ALBERS

"Reverse is the movement of Tao,
Yielding is the action of Tao."

—TAO TE CHING

Yanger than Springtime

Muse on the Tai Ji symbol . . . . Let it spin and rotate in your mind (and with your head). Like a top or a coin, a sphere or a bubble . . . .

The line through the center is wavy to perpetuate movement—like a flowing watercourse, not a permanently enforced division.

Its meaning is in its movement, in its dance of fluid change. Do not let it become fixed as you watch it. Let it dance its dance of unity and separateness, of sameness and difference—now so much one that it becomes the other. Yang and yin and back to yang . . . which is which?

Exactly!

Neither yang nor yin is a fixed state of being. Trying to be more of one to the exclusion of the other creates an excess that defeats itself. "Too yang" could be called macho;

44

"too yin," marshmallow. The first, in its unyielding rigidity, falls to the wind, which readily finds the weakness in too much strength. The second, in its limpness—like overcooked noodles—creates a tyranny of helplessness.

To strengthen the yang of the oak, mix in some yin of young bamboo. Dance on both feet, balance the advancing and the yielding, the stepping down and the picking up. Allow spring to emerge from winter's grip and turn into the sere of summer, which is cooled by autumn's quickening breeze.

Now, look at another variation of the Tai Ji symbol with an empty circle in the center . . . .

What do we have here? A "white" hole?! Could it be the ultimate "vacuum" that contains all there is to be contained? Or the Still Point!

Watch it spin and rotate more . . . .

Sprinkle the salt (the white dots on yin) and the pepper (the black spots on yang) to spice up the mixture. Increase the dynamic range and variations of the *yanger* and *yinner* dancing.

Dance on . . . .

The Original Face Before You Were Born

—To be transparent for the transcendence!

In Chinese classical theater, the treacherous characters blank out their faces with white paint to disguise their "true colors." Others use a spectrum of multicolored designs to accentuate the characteristics of their true selves. In everyday drama we portray the variations of our *personae* and change our masks for the different roles we play as readily as the best actors on stage.

So what is mask and what is face? Which is your true face? The one you present at work? At home with your loved ones? The one in the mirror when you are alone?

The Zen priest Hoshi of T'ang dynasty China, in deep meditation, peeled back his face from the middle only to reveal yet another face beneath.

How many layers has your face? Peel the onion. And yet again.

What face do you have at the heart?

Egg on My Face

The comic characters of Chinese theater have a white triangular spot right over the nose. Its origin is an ancient joke about someone looking heavenward—and getting a bird dropping right on the face. To learn to carry that ignoble prize and make it something to grin about is an achievement.

We have all suffered when our inflated egos received an inevitable direct hit.

I had just finished delivering to a celebrated sports symposium what I considered to be one of my best lecture-demonstrations. My ego-balloon was soaring high. Then appeared a well-known new age figure to entice me into one of his "new games," touted as joyful, noncompetitive mutual experiences.

With both of us intensely aware of our celebrity status before the assembled onlookers, we began tossing a raw egg back and forth as we gradually increased the distance between us. The game demands the ability to catch the egg gently, yielding with the impact so it will not break. The task becomes increasingly difficult as the distance is increased and the egg is thrown farther and higher. Sooner or later the egg has to break!

The showdown is that tense moment when you sense that the limit has been reached—the next catch is bound to be the last and you pray that the yolk will not be on you!

Of course, there is the choice of not trying to catch the egg, of simply letting it smash on the ground. But on that memorable day there was an audience egging us on. We *had* to continue trying the catch until—*splat!*

What a disrespectful mess! Egg all over the Tai Ji master's silk brocade jacket and on his conspicuous chagrin! Egg on my face and an unmistakable gleeful twinkle in my opponent's eye!

For several years the incident bothered me. It was a thorn in my ego. Now, finally, I have come to cherish that scene and its message about the value in risking egg on your face, literally and figuratively. Yes, I could have simply dodged the egg. Letting it fall would have saved face, not to mention the cleaning bill for my silk jacket. But what a meaningless story to tell!

I wear my white triangular spot with pride.

Remember when Tai Ji was still quite exotic in the Western world and many of its initiates showed off their novel skill with elaborate self-indulgence? One of my most resolute students was the epitome of this vanity. He was a handsome German aristocrat, artistic and sensitive, a man who dressed for maximum effect, exercised rigorously to keep "the body electric" fully charged, and fretted over his receding hairline. The discovery of Tai Ji seemed to soothe his anxiety over life's ephemeral beauty. So he practiced Tai Ji morning, noon, and night—anywhere and everywhere.

As Tai Ji became an obsession with him, it lost its center, so he pursued it even more intensely. In striving to hold on, he squeezed the life out of it. And still he clung.

Early one morning he was diligently performing his Tai Ji ritual in the park. A dog came along, sniffed as dogs do, then nonchalantly hoisted his leg and peed all over the expensively garbed leg and Gucchi shoes!

It was my student's private humiliation for a long time, until the day finally came when he told the story—to the merriment of all and to his own great relief. He realized that his Tai Ji must have been as rigid and inanimate as a fire hydrant. The dog was merely acknowledging and following its nature.

Had my student been dancing his Tai Ji with the rhythm of the moment instead of doggedly pursuing its forms, he could easily have shooed the dog away. Instead, the dog *shoed* him!

Maybe you have some symbolic bird-doo on your forehead or egg on your face or dog pee on your Guccis. Pretending it isn't there only spreads the muck further. Display it and enjoy it. Turn it into a badge of honor.

Feeling and Form

"It is difficult to be muddleheaded, and difficult to be intelligent. It is even more difficult to graduate from intelligence into muddleheadedness."
—CHEN PAN-CH'AO, artist-poet, Ch'ing dynasty

Mind and Matter
"Do you mind?" "No matter!"
"What's the matter?" "Never mind!"

Mind body Relish

—the Pattern Which Connects

In clear light, I take great pride and rejoice in my multi-disciplinary interest and experiences in life's learning. In confusion, I sometimes curse my "everything-in-the-kitchen-sink" chop-suey knowledge. Still, my thirst for the new and the unknown has always been unquenchable. I do thrive on challenges and delight in the transcendence, but the crux of this perennial yearning to break through is ever-present in the Tao—"the pattern which connects" *all!*

Epistemologist-philosopher Gregory Bateson, one of the most original and complex minds I have ever encountered, taught me to trust this pattern. When I first tried to read his book, *Steps to an Ecology of Mind,* I couldn't climb *his* steps to an ecology of *my* mind at all. His written words perplexed me. I felt like the "well-frog," frustrated at not seeing the sky beyond the rim of my confined opening.

The path to crossing the barrier began one summer when his twelve-year-old daughter, Nora, spent a month dancing Tai Ji with our group in Hawaii. Occasionally, when Nora wrote to her father, she'd ask me to add a line or two, and Gregory would reciprocate by writing something for me in his letters to Nora. Thus began a "metalogue," which made his language seem simple and easy: We merely talked.

Every time we met I became more and more aware that though his mind was performing intricate arabesques, his body was rigidly immobile. And I was self-consciously showing off the freedom of my dancing body to conceal my intimidated, sluggish mind. I was painfully aware of his awareness, and his conscious effort to conceal the knowing was glaringly awkward. What a double bind!

Heart Mind Om

But, gradually, as we let go of trying too hard, our mutual affection and the ease of being together made the eventual confession an occasion to celebrate. We both yearned for transcendence of our limitations, so we created a joint seminar. We called it: "Giant Dancing Steps to an Ecology of Mindbody." We drew a group of people eager and grateful to have it confirmed that the "dancing mind/thinking body" is a birthright for all.

This successful, historic week of learning ended with a finale of Gregory leading the group, with exuberance and no little grace, in high kicks to the music from *A Chorus Line*.

Shiva Dancing

"Follow Your Bliss!"

Right after celebrating his 80th birthday at the Palace of Fine Arts in San Francisco, Joseph Campbell and I drove down to the Esalen Institute in Big Sur to conduct our annual collaboration on the MYTHBODY.

The spectacular coast highway unraveled before us with the magnificent azure sky above, emerald mountains to the left, and the limpid Pacific Ocean forever expanding on the right. Occasionally, migrating whales returning north would spout rainbow fountains in the sunset. Joseph sighed with joy, then exclaimed ecstatically, "This IS magnificent . . . my body and all my senses are saying, 'THIS IS IT!' But why is it my mind keeps asking, 'WHERE IS THE LIBRARY?'. . ."

When asked, "What is your meditation?" Campbell was known to reply in perfect candor, "Underlining sentences." In spite of the fact that he was a world class athlete and a fine saxophone player in his college days, Joe had always been more at ease reading and dancing with his mind than with his body. Yet for eight consecutive years of Joseph's birthday week, when we were together in Big Sur exploring and experimenting with our enthusiastic seminarians on the continual integration of

56

Body, Mind and Spirit, we both became increasingly convinced that the human body was, indeed, the ultimate myth.

Each year we assembled two distinctly split groups; the Campbellian thinker-intellectuals who ignored the overt expressiveness of the body, and the Tai Ji feeler-movers who resisted words and abstractions. But always, as the week moved on and Joe and I began to integrate and synthesize, the distinction between the two groups would fade and eventually melt into one. We danced with our minds and cogitated with our bodies, day by day becoming one harmonious unity. The symbolic imagery of the "Dancing Shiva" would inevitably be mimed, led by Joseph hopping about on one leg, with nimble hands and arms gesticulating the appropriate mudras. His famous Kundalini lecture, with those potent visual images shining through the projection lanterns, would be immediately translated into our bodies in deep, visceral experiences.

Joseph was quick to realize his initial reluctance to physical expression and showed us, with heroic passion and humility, how easily we all could manage to expand our capacities and deepen our consciousness in multiple dimensions. To be Body-Mind-Spirit in harmonious whole must be on top of our list in the search for our ultimate bliss. Once found, follow it!

Shangri-la on the San Andreas Fault

Alan Watts once wanted to use the title "Shangri-la on the San Andreas Fault" for a seminar he was giving at an institute on California's Big Sur coastline. However, the management decided it was unwise to advertise their proximity to the famous fault and changed the title to "Shangri-la at the Edge of the Sea." Exit Paradox, enter non sequitur.

Alan's point, of course, was that for true peace of mind we must acknowledge whatever fault we live upon, whatever time bomb ticks in our closet, and enjoy our Shangri-la nonetheless. It is not the absence of the problem; it is how one lives in its presence that matters.

I had read Alan's book *The Wisdom of Insecurity* and admired it in an abstract manner until he brought its point home to me directly. He insisted I not only accept my insecurity in the English language but *use* it. "Don't you dare improve your Chinese-English," he said. "Look at me. I am so clever with words that I trick myself all the time. I can turn it off and on, like a taped message, always slick and perfect. No, you just keep fumbling. The essence is better conveyed that way."

Alan was essentially shy, extremely critical of himself, yet he developed into a flamboyant and gregarious man. His enjoyment of life was based on his open acknowledgment of all the faults webbing the ground beneath him. He was Buddha with feet of clay, yet those feet were firmly placed on the way.

Through him I recognize that shortcomings make light baggage if they are openly accepted.

Banana Split 'ala Ch'i

"The latest incarnation of Oedipus, the continued romance of Beauty and the Beast, stands this afternoon on the corner of 42nd Street and Fifth Avenue, waiting for the traffic light to change." This, Joseph Campbell's vivid description of modern-day mythology, always gives me a tremendous lift.

Too quickly do we outgrow belief in ancient myths, childhood fantasies, and fairy tales; too quickly do we discredit Santa Claus, the Easter bunny, and the tooth fairy. And we feel lost and our souls vacant, watching our imaginations weaken and our minds and bodies wither unnecessarily into apathetic senility.

Children are openly willing to believe in the magic and mystery of the energy force around us and within us. Some say that's because they are especially naive, others because they are especially wise.

My young daughters were delighted with the movie *Star Wars* and its sequels. Now at last they had an answer to the questions from their friends about what their daddy did: "He teaches the *force!*"

No matter, children are more open than jaded adults to the demonstration of *ch'i,* the energy of the universe and of each simple breath you take. The very breath of life. The powerful *force* unforced. They have no problem with *miracles,* big or small!

I grew up in China believing in Taoist immortals and their godlike transcendence from human bondage. Many times during my childhood I threatened to leave home to become an apprentice to the O-Mei Mountain immortals in Szechuan. Once, my brother and I followed the instructions from a secret book by gradually adding weight to our shoes, believing that if we continued this practice for five years, we would be able to step out of our shoes and fly! (Alas, we never managed beyond the first month, by which time we sounded like a Chinese counterpart of Dickens's Christmas ghost dragging iron chains from purgatory.) Still, some fantasy persists today in my life and in my daily Tai Ji practice.

The following personal tidbit of my family fun may seem corny and childish at first, but if you allow yourself to play with us, you may find a rejuvenation and reawaken a long-lost *sense of awe!* I will let you decide whether it is merely "metaphorical" or "real".

Whenever we have cold cereal for breakfast, we each bridge a bright yellow banana across our cereal bowls. We are going to honor the ceremony of banana splitting. Solemnly, my daughters and I dance our Tai Ji motifs, generating our *ch'i* through the five elements—fire, water, wood, metal, earth. Centered and focused with mounting energy, we elevate to stand on our chairs directly over our bowls and deliver remote karate chops at the bananas.

Quietly and confidently we then sit down to our bowls, peel the bananas, and allow the neatly sliced segments to roll on the cereal!

Why don't you try something as simply magical as this at your next breakfast table?

"May the *force* be with you always!"

Are you what you Eat or

Many people assume that I am a vegetarian, but I am not. Oh, I have gone down the tofu and miso path, searching for that purity of diet, just as I have sought a purity of soul. But I am resigned to being an imperfect sage and I eat accordingly.

Chinese cooking is highly varied and I take pleasure in that variety. Meat is used selectively and sparingly. When I first came to the United States, a big naked chunk of beef made me gag. But with practice and determination to become a "real American," I discovered that an occasional steak could be a treat. I am an eclectic as well as a hearty eater.

My new students are often convinced that "I am what I eat." I am asked repeatedly about my diet. I sometimes retort with this fable:

An orphaned tiger cub is brought up by a benign herd of goats in their vegetarian ways. Does the tiger remain naively satisfied with his salads, bleating thanksgiving for his daily fare? Or will he one day realize that just because he lives among goats does not *make* him a goat?

I let them complete the rest of the scenario.

Do you Eat who you are?

I would rather that people did not take their food so seriously. But when they do, I respect it. At our resident workshops, we see that vegetarian meals are available. Sometimes we make very erroneous presumptions. For instance:

Lama Anagarika Govinda was to conduct seminars at a weeklong retreat. Diligently, those at the center set about stocking their kitchen with sprouts and tofu and juices and fruits and assorted veggie delicacies. When Lama Govinda arrived, guess what he asked for? Pizza, spaghetti, and sugar cookies.

The grapevine around Boston has it that the leading macrobiotic diet guru of the world has been seen hanging out at a Dunkin' Donuts!

After his usual brilliant lecture on the kundalini, Joseph Campbell was approached by a seeker certain that the Campbellian vibrant health and keen mind after nearly eight decades on this earth must be attributable to a special diet. His secret? "Rare roast beef and good Irish whiskey," Joseph boomed.

Hot Croissants Cool Carrots

Most of us are susceptible to fads—or else there would be no fads! We sip Perrier water, wear only Birkenstock sandals, or become croissant connoisseurs—until we recognize ourselves as living stereotypes lampooned by the current *New Yorker* cartoons. Something urges us to be the first on our block to try some new dietary delight or vacation paradise and to know firsthand all that *Vogue* magazine tells us "People are talking about . . . . "

In my thirty years of teaching in the "growth"-conscious new world, I have been exposed to a rich diet of the newest and latest ways to become authentic, realized, clear, adjusted, open, and/or complete. Look in any of the "new age" catalogues and you will find the menu for an endless banquet. If you insist on trying all the dishes, you will be sure to develop an upset stomach and a bloated head—or vice versa.

Still, the compulsion to try it all—often wearing the robes of the search—is strong. I am thinking now of two people vying for the unofficial championship of Workshops-Taken-for-Self-Improvement. One counted one hundred and fifty in four years, and he is still as mixed up as a bucket of magenta paint.

To follow every trend and sample every new therapy will only satisfy a superficial acquisitiveness—the "I have been to," "I have studied with," "I have had," bragging rights. Maybe it would be more fruitful to pause and ask yourself what real nourishment you are getting from such a smorgasbord rather than counting up the weeks of workshops.

The price you pay for a Norwalk juicer might encourage you to drink your carrot juice with greater respect, but it is still the juice that matters. It is the way you allow your body to absorb the essence of the carrot that counts, not how much time, money, and effort you expended to make the juice.

Croissants, like fads, are delicious for a few hot instants. But need we rush to sample them all? New buns are featured daily!

Tossed I Ching Salad

When, as a child, I began the study of the *I Ching*, I understood very little of its meaning, but its oracle aspects appealed to me greatly. The ceremony involved in consulting the *I Ching* was most mysterious and theatrical, and I never grew tired of performing it.

When the *I Ching* became chic in the sixties, I was a bit embarrassed by the glib and glossy interpretations of its "ancient Chinese secrets." But still I enjoyed the reflected attention cast on me as a supposed expert. To show off and be "right on," I willingly cast the coins.

When I wished to pad my part, I used the yarrow stalk method just to be one-up on the mere coin throwers. I elaborately gathered and sorted the yarrow stalks. After a time I felt a vague uneasiness that the theatricality was becoming mere show biz and all too slick and cliché.

Then, when the one-too-many flower children asked me: "Hey, man, do you throw the *I Ching?*" (usually mispronouncing it as "eye ching") I retorted: "Yes, I throw the *I Ching . . . . out!*"

Looking back, I begin to understand my answer. I wanted to throw *my Ching* out—the easy showiness of the game—and enter back into *the Ching*. I wanted to open the curtain to the true theater and close the curtain on my performance.

As I grow older with the *I Ching*, I find more joy and gratification, learning to partake gradually of its perennial wisdom in small dosages. I enjoy chewing on bite-size morsels day by day, savoring and digesting my understanding slowly. It is reassuring to realize that Confucius had only begun to appreciate the true value of the *I Ching* after reaching the ripe age of seventy. What is our hurry? The yarrow is not stalking us.

Sun

Change
Sun
and
Moon
Alternating

A transforming
Chameleon

Moon
Sunglow

ॐ

AHA
HA

Hearts of Mantras

"Why in Illinois?" people keep asking when I tell them where I live. They assume I live in some dramatic place with the sea pounding below my feet or mountains towering over my head. "Why there?"

"For the corn." I laugh. But I mean it. Although people on the coasts may be more searching, more questing, more immediately interesting, I find that the corn-growing farmer-philosophers of Middle America have roots firmly planted and heads squarely on their shoulders.

The sun rises and sets every bit as golden on the Heartland as it does over oceans. And I find a settledness in the Midwest that I like coming home to. Usually, I have been flying all over the globe, here and there, and I like coming to ground. I need it. The fact that things don't move so swiftly in the country's great midsection is a comfort to me. It is refreshing to come back to the still-point after the storm of my travels.

One day, while driving along an uneventful Kansas highway, filled with a mysterious calm, I spotted a road-side sign to the effect: "You are at the Midpoint of the United States." Aha! I laughed, the gut-belly-*hara tant'ien* of America, the country's very *center*.

Imagine passing through the monochromic landscape of Nebraska, inhaling the invigorating scent of the stockyards, and seeing signs for Omaha. OM—AHA! OM, OM on the range!

The *Heart*land! Country roads, take me OM!

For Name

While in high school in China, my two elder brothers respectively picked Alexander (the Great!) and Frederick (another Great!) for their Western names. They thought Alfred would be good for me. Even though I told them I was much more enamored by Gene, as in Kelly, and Groucho, as in Marx, my brothers persuaded me that I must pay homage to the doctor who once saved my life in a missionary hospital, Dr. Alfred E. Newman.

Although I came to America with a passport that spelled Huang Chung-liang, my Western friends improvised with such Alfred-esques as Alec, Albert, Alfonse, Alfredo, even Alyosha and Ali Baba. And finally, Al, for short!

I was resigned to being Al to all but a few earnest acquaintances until recently in Bombay when an Indian friend confessed to me, "Every time I call you Al, I think of that gangster in Chicago!"

Now I request all my friends to keep trying with Chung (Tzong)-Liang (Leeang). My name consists of two inspiring characters:

CHUNG: CENTERED
HEART-MIND

LIANG: ORIGINAL QUALITIES OF
PURE WHITE CRYSTALS

Why would I settle for being only Al?
Why would you settle for Al?
Why would anyone?

MOUNTAIN ORCHID

FOREST MOSS

These are the names of my two daughters, Yulan and Tysan. They are the joy of my life, the "dim sum" learning of my daily living.

When we picked the names for them, we wished for them the qualities for a lifelong self-cultivation. To bloom in the deep interior of the mountain for oneself (not for others to see) is the essence of Yulan (mountain orchid). To be humble and subtle in manifestation yet invincible and expansive as the moss in the forest, Tysan.

71

At twenty, Yulan still prefers her American name, Lark. She does bloom like the orchid however, absorbing people, places and knowledge like aerial roots, into the strength of the mountain within her.

At sixteen, Tysan is a Leo-tiger (born of the month and year) who runs surefooted through the forest, tripping on occasional teenage rocks but rebounding with steadfast resilience and grace. Her roots spread slowly and tenaciously.

They are my teachers for life! Perhaps they were given their names as an intuitive desire to cultivate those qualities in my *own* life.

I relish my travels and my public life. I take great pride and pleasure in my ability to reach out to and be touched by so many. But I know I am paying a considerable price for this jet-age rhythm. Tysan informed me matter-of-factly long ago that she loved Mommy more than me, simply because "Mommy is always *here,* and you are *gone* a lot!" That hurts. But she made me look closely at my cluttered calendar and manage to pencil in blocks of time to *be home!* I must learn clearly the difference between the "orchid in the mountain" flowering for its own nature and the "showroom orchid" to be admired by a crowd.

I remain chagrined by Lark's three-year-old willful protest, "If you're going to play with me, *do* it! If you're not, *don't!*" Often, I still fail to distinguish, like the moss, quality from quantity, and the trees from the forest!

Singing Suz-annie's Song

My wife, Suzanne, teases me that she is "comfortable" with me. But I yearn for melodrama!

After twenty-five years, two children, and many storms, we manage to remain, simply, a couple. Our "special" secret? None. We shuffle and stumble the same way all couples do.

As we look around, we see other couples working *very* hard at being *couples,* often taking the natural swing out of their relationships. Perhaps a thriving partnership is not built only on special-effort romance and fireworks. It may depend on not-so-special, day-to-day events.

Yet it never seems enough just to be "cozy" with each other! We need to stir up our adrenaline from time to time, to rekindle our passions with flowers and/or battles. These moments are wonderful and spectacular, but they are ephemeral, like snowflakes. A few days later we are once again *comfortable* with each other and ready to settle in—until the next sudden wave of anxiety.

For us, these cycles seem to come naturally. Since we seldom know when to expect these waves, so far Suzanne and I have *never yet* had to work on keeping up with them.

73

All
Wontons
Look
Alike

America is a big melting pot. We are truly a chop-suey country with a rainbow spectrum of races, religions, and ethnic uniqueness.

Quick! Think of a joke. Most of them will probably turn out to be ethnic, religious, or sexual—our favorite taboo topics of suppression and confusion.

I have learned to enjoy my own stereotypes. Imagine me, a just-off-the-boat foreign student, playing Curly, the cowboy, in the college production of *Oklahoma!* Starry-eyed after that, I strutted to Hollywood to audition for *West Side Story*. Surprisingly, no one seemed to notice that the spunky kid in the front row was an Oriental until the final round of eliminations.

My consolation prize was to be seen and chosen by Sammy Davis for his one-man show. I was a natural for his *color*ful jokes, pairing my yellow with his black.

Next I "Ching-Ching Chinaman-ed" my way through *Flower Drum Song* and had an ephemeral TV fling in the "Green Hornet" with Bruce Lee.

Now, more than thirty years later, I watch the late, late reruns of that period of my life with my daughters. They get uproariously silly watching me. I get egg foo yung on my face when they say, "Hey, Dad! You were *realll* cute!"

"Were?" Thanks a lot!

WON

TON

"CLOUD-SWALLOWING" GOOD!

Running overtime, I had just finished taping a samurai sword dance for an NBC-TV "China Special" when my sister appeared to present me with a beautiful tailored Chinese army coat she had brought back for me from my father. With no time and no room left in my suitcase, I decided to wear the coat to catch the plane home from the Los Angeles Airport. I was immediately seized by four security officers and whisked away for interrogation about possible "samurai hijacking"! They confessed that I looked a wee bit suspicious with my slanty eyes, wearing my father's army coat, and wielding a long sword!

My mother is very popular with my Occidental friends and students. They dote on her and affectionately call her Mama Huang. They write to her and visit her at her Los Angeles apartment. But Mama Huang confesses to me that she is often embarrassed because she cannot tell them apart.

During a period of increased neighborhood crime, she wisely double-locked and chained her front door. When callers came to the door, she examined them cautiously through the peephole. To be sure that the person was a genuine Tai Ji friend, she would bellow with great gusto to test them. The familiar friends knew how to reciprocate with a similar "*Ho-ho*" and "Aha-ha" and "Mama Huang"!

There were two or three occasions, however, when she witnessed the callers jump with alarm and retreat very hastily. "If they don't know how to roar from their *tant'ien*," she assured me, "they are worthless students for you anyway!"

My friend Fritjof Capra and I both found ourselves in Hong Kong at the same time. We arranged to meet at a concert one night. Halfway through the evening he finally managed to find me in the crowd, but he was embarrassed to admit that compared to my usual distinctive appearance at events in the West, I seemed to have blended into this "all-Oriental" sea of faces!

Prejudice runs on both halves of the sphere. When my oldest sister married a blond American, my father disowned her. She was wise enough to return home when she was seven months pregnant. And my father embraced her (and his new-to-be first grandchild), with all grudges erased.

My parents-in-law were brought up in a straight-laced, self-righteous, tiny Midwestern town. Like everyone else, they were forced to consider "What will the town say?"

When they announced their daughter's impending marriage, the hometown was in quite a stir. For weeks it clucked and debated Suzanne's descent into shame. Naturally, her parents didn't jump up and down with joy at the startling news either. They realized they were trapped in the non-choice of defending their daughter's nonconformity. And valiantly defend and accept it they did!

A bit of support came from an unexpected source. At a heated discussion of the weekly church social, an upright and no-nonsense, feisty dowager stood up and firmly announced: "If Moses can marry an Ethiopian, Suzanne can marry a Chinaman."

And my mother-in-law reassuringly added that the wedding was to take place in a Methodist church—in Chinatown!

When we were newly married and feeling passionately glued together, Suzanne hesitantly took her first leave from me to visit her sister for a weekend. The day she returned, I rushed home after work to greet her open-armed at the doorway. She looked up, startled. "Oh, my God, you're *Chinese!*"

When Alan Watts and I conducted seminars together, I always made it a point to dress overtly Occidental. With Alan's habitual fondness for all things Asian, I thought one Oriental between the two of us was quite sufficient. I appeared on one occasion to discuss and demonstrate the art of the tea ceremony in my Western getup, complete with boots and hat. Appropriately, the only equipment we could acquire for that afternoon was a snorting coffee maker and plastic cups and utensils. We found great pleasure in the incongruity of his green-eyed Zen master and my yellow-skinned cowboy meticulously going through the ritual of creating "beauty and essence" in spite of the mixed-up cultural juxtapositions.

Suzanne, blue-eyed and fair-skinned, was definitely a standout the year we lived in Taiwan. I would consciously avoid her company whenever I wished to be just one of the crowd. We mutually agreed that she stay "a few paces behind" during our shopping outings. When we were seen together, my bargaining power diminished drastically.

One day we were together trying to arrive at a fair price with a taxi driver. He gave me the disdainful glare usually reserved for gigolos or foreign tourists' "running dogs." Shortly after we got into the cab (a bumpy ride indeed), the driver realized we were husband and wife. He turned around and beamed from ear to ear. "Why didn't you say so? If she's your wife, then she's Chinese, too! I will take you both home for free!"

Return
to
One
Two
Three

(Return to One Two Three)

The *One Stroke* in Chinese writing is the most basic *core*.
One contains all—the *Whole*.
The *One*-stroke is the *Hologram*.
It contains all the *ch'i*-energy force of the universe.
All the meaning there *is*.

Two Strokes begin the relationship, the dualism-polarity, the yang and yin, between heaven and earth, between two human beings.
The empty space between two solid lines.
The complementary lengths balancing the two *ones:* The longer, more solid, earth-line supporting the shorter, lighter heaven-line.

Three Strokes spin a new interrelationship—A *Trio*.

      The middle stroke symbolizes the *human* between heaven (upper line) and earth (lower line). Man, the intermediary between heaven and earth. The eternal triad.

      It becomes the first of eight trigrams to form the *I Ching*.

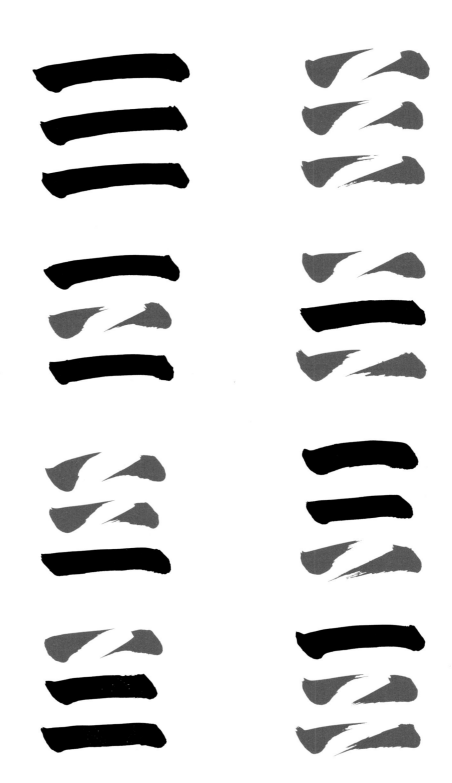

Maybe you've heard the story of the two psychiatrists meeting each other in a hallway. "Hello," says one in passing. "I wonder what he meant by that?" thinks the other.

That seems to be what's happening to the messages in the *I Ching*. There are more interpretations, explanations of the interpretations, and commentaries on the explanations than there is *I Ching*! No wonder the West thinks the East inscrutable.

The Chinese call unnecessary adornment "putting legs on snakes." That's what we are doing when we laboriously try to link the fragments in the *I Ching* or dogmatically force linear logic out of the random parts of the whole.

Chuang Tzu told us that when we catch the fish, forget the net. Alan Watts updated that with, "When you get the message, hang up the phone."

Let's get back to the basics—the unadorned hexagrams themselves. All sixty-four of them are made up of simple strokes—either two short lines making up one line or one longer one.

Look at the strokes. Think of what we know about holograms—a *whole* made up of parts and each part containing the whole. Cut up the hologram and each segment has all the total information.

So it is with the hexagram. Break it into parts—the lines and strokes. Let these strokes stand on their own. Let the smallest part tell you the whole story. Sense the energy in the brush strokes. Notice the bold and the not-so-bold. See the pockets made by their combinations. Some are open to the sky, some to the ground; some are contained, some are moving onward.

Group them in twos and threes and in fours and sixes. See the relationships. Look to them for your message. Allow your own wisdom to be triggered by these symbols.

Use a brush to draw the lines. You will instantly sense the energy in the self-written calligraphic version. Feel the power from the brush strokes. See beyond and under the surface.

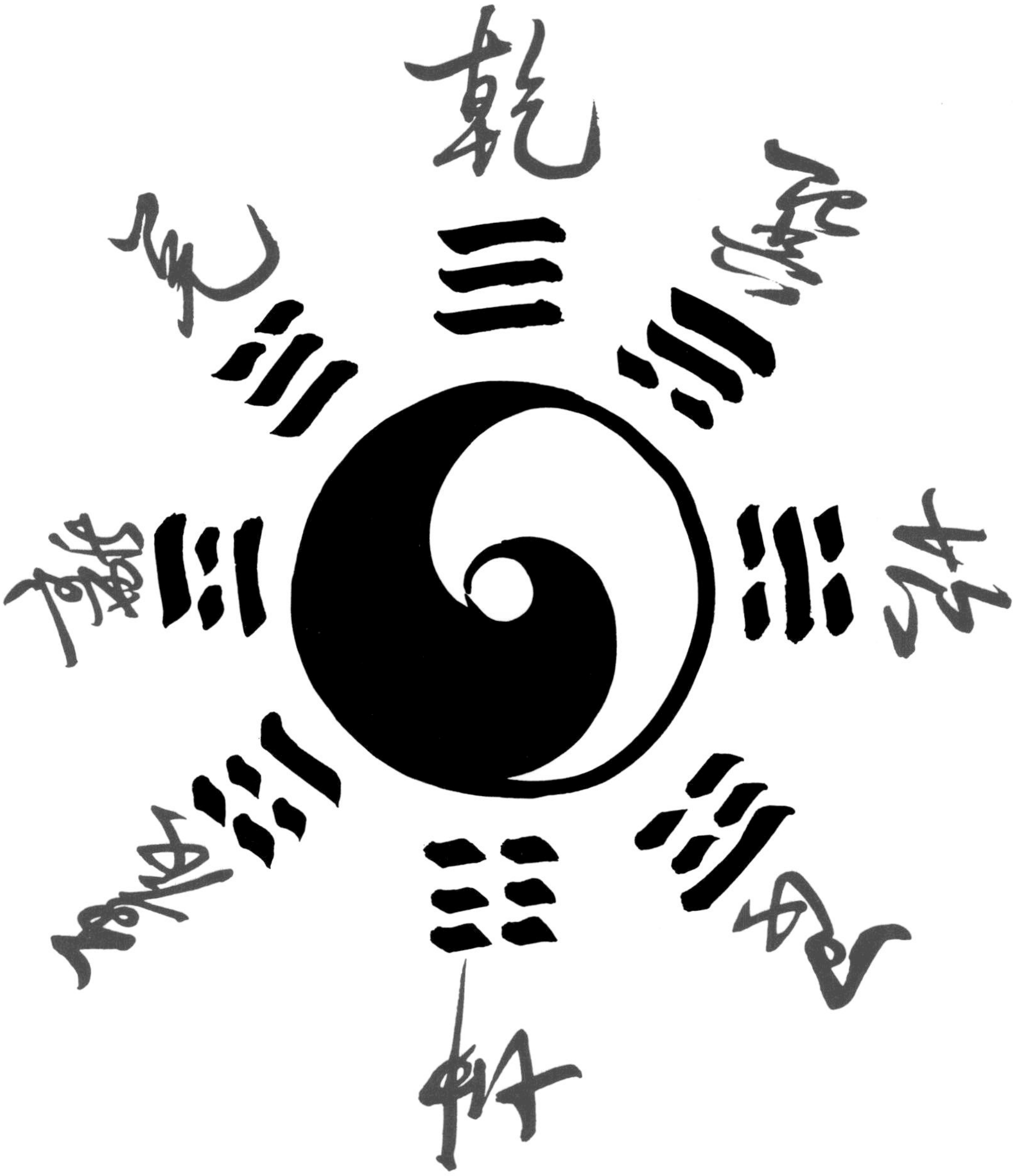
乾

Pieces of Eight

If you find it difficult to remember these eight trigrams, or four pairs of yin-yang triads, try to experience them in the following simple exercises.

Clasp your hands with palms outward and raise them overhead. Keep pulling on your hands but maintain the grip to feel the inertia of the force. This represents the top one-stroke, heaven, or a yang energy line. Next, bring the clasped hands to the level of your solar plexus, midrange (heart) in the torso. This represents the middle line, the human yang power within the trigram. Finally, bring the clasped hands down to the belly, still pulling, feeling the inertia, to represent the lower one-stroke, the earth with all the intrinsic heaven-yang energy force.

You have just experienced the first trigram, *Ch'ien,* with three one-strokes of yang energy, symbolizing heaven, the creative, masculine, sun, day, father, external power, and so on.

Now, repeat the same three positions with your clasped hands, except each time, after feeling the inertia, you release the grip overhead, then down in front of the solar plexus, and finally open at the belly. Each time, allow the inert potency to come forth. They represent the three yin lines, which form the second trigram *K'un,* to complement the *Ch'ien,* with qualities of earth, the receptive, feminine, moon, night, mother, intrinsic wisdom . . . .

The next pair of trigrams is *Li* (fire) and *K'an* (water). For fire, maintain the clasp overhead as well as at the belly. Then release the center grip to show the hollow of the fire power. Open and let the fire come out!

Water trigram works in the reverse, with the grip maintained at the heart to express the inner strength of the water, but release the grips at overhead and at the belly for fluidity.

87

The next are *Chên* (thunder) and *Sun* (wind).

Begin the pulling at the gut level for thunder, but release the force as it explodes upward when you reach the middle and above your head. Let go of your grips with a thunderous shout.

Reverse the pattern to contain the potential force on top and in the middle, but release at the gut to show the movement of the flowing, sweeping wind upon earth.

The final pair are *Tui* (mountain lake) and *Kên* (mountain still-ness). Begin the lake exercise from the belly (*tant'ien*) with solid clasp of your hands, then move up to chest level, still pul-ling, and finally release your hands like a mountain, opening to the sky.

Reverse this process. Begin with the overhead heav-enly yang grip, then move downward to open at the middle. And continue to open from the belly. This downward opening sug-gests a return to the earth, a solid mountain of our own stance, the stillness and comfort of home.

We move on to the sixty-four variations by playing the matching game of coupling these three-line metaphoric symbols. Often these intrinsic meanings of the hexagrams can be understood at a glance.

When we hide the sun *Li* under/behind the earth *K'un*, we conceal the source (heat and glare) of the sun. Therefore, the hexagram *Ming I* literally means "obscuring the light." But the variable applications of the core change with the individual observation in time and space.

During the last complete moon eclipse, I experienced a temporal "total darkness." I realized that even the all-eternal glow of the sun once in a while hides behind the earth to provide us another view of the moon without sun's interference. An enlightening lesson in *Wu wei*—the art of inaction, getting out of the way!

In yet another aspect of practical learning from this hexagram, we recognize the wisdom in dimming our personal glow from time to time. Luminous moments are wonderfully ego-boosting, but all "luminaries" must learn to dim their glaring aura appropriately to avoid overexposure.

"First he ascends high up in the sky, illuminating the four quarters of the earth! Beware of transgression and losing the Way; he then plunges into the depths of the earth in darkness!"

—*I Ching* commentary on *Ming I*
(Six line at the top)

In the *I Ching,* this hexagram explains the phenomenon of moon eclipse—*Ming I* (#36), Obscuring the Light. We see that the sun (*Li*) hides under/behind the earth (*K'un*) to obscure its light on the moon.

The Way
of
The Brush

During my years of study in the United States, my parents insisted that I write to them with my Chinese brush. I remember resenting them for making me spend extra time to prepare the ink and maintain my calligraphic practice. I preferred to whisk off a quick ballpoint-pen letter and have more time for study and social life.

Now I recognize their wisdom.

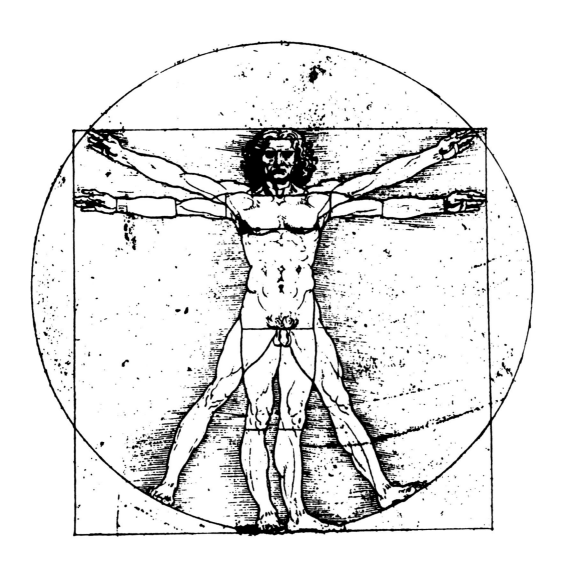

If I had never left China and hadn't learned another tongue I probably would not be able to look upon my native written language with such renewed joy and respect. Now I see the Chinese characters as symbols of meaning far beyond the words they stand for. I am sure that it is my removal in time and distance from my origins that makes this possible.

Today the deep meanings of the ancient characters bubble up through the superficial word-level definitions. I am constantly surprised and delighted as I practice my calligraphy at the revelations that spring to the surface. There, emerging in black and white from my brush, are things so often seen before yet never recognized, that I leap with excitement. My brush dances ever faster, and my whole body dances to express the dark strokes and the white spaces with and around me.

Sometimes I become so excited that I race ahead of my class with lots of "Oh, look at this! And see that!" But enough students follow my enthusiasm to make such a session deeply rewarding.

For instance, the character for big or great (大) shows a person with wide-open arms and legs—the Chinese version of the DaVinci-Vitruvius man.

to Emptiness

The word for *Tai,* as in Tai Ji, is simply the great human with an additional "centering in the *tant'ien*" belly stroke.

We jump to our feet and dance the character. We fling our arms open, connect our energy from head to toe in exuberant sweeping leg kicks, and stir the fire energy in our *tant'ien*, wrapping and slapping on our bellies with gutsy *Ha-ha!!*

And the character for heaven, or sky, is the additional one-stroke placed above "the great human." We dance the wide-open arm gesture to behold the heaven spirit and receive it like a funnel, shouting Chinese *T'ien!*

Sometimes in my teaching I go back and forth from the simple strokes of *I Ching* hexagrams to various revealing characters. For example, to better understand the meaning of "the gate to all mystery" from *Lao Tzu*, I write the Chinese character for *gate—Men*.

It looks rather like a swinging door in an old Western saloon, doesn't it? It is clearly an entrance. (Or an exit.) Remember that the way *in* is the way *out* is the way *in* . . . .

Now look at the first two hexagram in *I Ching*.

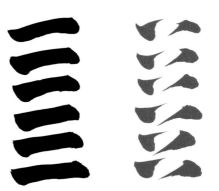

On the right, *K'un*, with six pairs of shorter lines, is actually a transformation of the hexagram *Ch'ien* on the left.

Cleave sharply through the center of *Ch'ien*, splitting all six strokes in the heart, and *K'un* is born.

This division represents both *Ch'ien* from *outer form* to *inner form* of *K'un*—from the solid to the void. The space in the center opens like a gate.

Look again into the new space just opened. Sense the energy moving through and emerging from it, circulating.

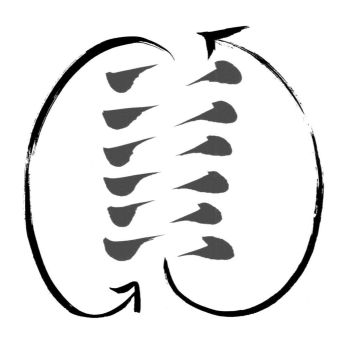

This is the essence of *emptiness*, which is pregnant with potential. It is an emptiness that contains all possibilities. It is a lively place of mystery and growth.

"All is emptiness; emptiness is all" is not a despairing thought in the Tao. Quite the opposite. Emptiness is the blank page on which anything can be written, the empty cup into which anything can be poured. It is the source.

Modern physics is catching up with this idea. "Theoretical and experimental physicists are now studying nothing at all—the vacuum. But that nothingness contains all of being," commented Heinz Pagels in *The Cosmic Code*. Science is coming into correspondence with the mystical awareness of the Oriental concepts of *Wu* (and *Yu*)—a nothing that means "no-thing," not "nothin.'"

The character for *Wu* (no-thing, nonbeing) () may seem complex at first glance, but once you can picture the brush strokes as "the clearing after a natural forest fire," then you can appreciate the overgrown "cluttered woods,"

and the fire burning below,

to experience the event.

The character *Yu* (thing, being, have . . .) () is the polar balance of *Wu*. Originally it depicted a primeval hand holding a chunk of meat.

Later, it evolved poetically into holding the moon in one's hand.

Finally, we have this.

Lao Tzu mused: "Out of nonbeing comes being. Out of the name-less comes all that is named in heaven and earth. As ever empty, we may perceive its inner essence; as ever manifest, we may realize its mystery . . . . However diverse, all flow from the same source . . . . Within the original mystery is a deeper mystery . . . and the gate opens, again and again . . . . "*

And the gate in the hexagram and in the character *Men* stands ready to open to our touch, to reveal the mysteries of the ancient world, the mysteries of modern science, and *ourselves*. All stem from nothingness, the fruitful emptiness beyond and within the gate.

*It is enlightening to recall those similar messages in Genesis of the Bible and other passages of holy scriptures of wisdom.

mi

Ch'i   Hides & Seek

Eight Precious Rice

One of the essential Chinese words is (米) mi—which, in design and symbolism, stands for the "eight cardinal directions" or "the eight natural phenomena." It also simply means "rice," the staple diet of more than half the world's population.

Let's look at the character as a sort of cosmic code, a blueprint to the very mysteries of the universe.

First, look at the center. We see a cross, the four directions. Within the four quadrants of the cross, on the diagonals, we see the four major forces coming toward and moving away from center. The upper two strokes gather from heaven above, aiming inward toward the spine-center; the lower two balancing strokes pour the energy out from the heart into the earth.

This "eight precious rice" character appears as the core, or "radical," in the written word *ch'i*, the élan vital. Surround the "eight precious" symbol with a dragonlike breath stroke (气), the dance of life begins.

Let's take this "eight cardinal directions" on a boat ride. Set it on top of the watercourse way stroke, (之). What do we have? A word meaning variously "searching for the eight phenomena" or "carried off by the river of life in eight directions." It also means "getting lost" (if you are not a good navigator) and becomes "hide-and-seek" (if you are enjoying the getting lost).

Tao Dung

—A Stink of Tao!

To preserve the reverence of the Tao, we often utilize some of its most irreverent aspects.

After a month of intense study of the Tao, a long-time student contributed to the class his satori of the day: "Tao is full of shit!" I immediately wrote down the Chinese character "excrement" and discovered much of the Tao in its components. Translated directly, this "substance of daily return to the earth" is composed of three radicals:

 Rice, converging/dispersing energy from eight cardinal points

 Field, earth divisions, brain, stomach, gut

 Commune, compose, coming together

We combined and connected these meanings and meditated on the synthesis of all the parts for the rest of the day with delight. From then on, Tao Dung became a frequent expression to warn us of our intellectual attachment to a lot of "verbal diarrhea"!

It was also great fun to pun the sound of Tao Dung to an everyday Chinese expression meaning literally "to smash the yoke," or "to stir up the egg!" It is used to describe mischief, delightful childlike pranks. Tao Dung is the divine prankster in each and every one of us. To recognize Tao Dung is to smell the Tao in its most sublime and ridiculous manifestations.

Tao is in everything, in the *food* and in the *Dung*. Don't pretend that it's sterile and plastic. Chew the living Tao well and learn to *dung* the deadly waste.

Fry Me to the Moon

Should the question arise: It is the Japanese who have trouble with the English *l* sound. They convert it to *r*, as in "rots of ruck." It is the Chinese who have trouble with the English *r* sound. They convert it to *l*, as in "flied lice." (Yet it is the Japanese actress, Miyoshi Umeki, star of *Sayonara*, who sings Julie London's torch song as "Cly Me a Liver.")

As a student at "UCRA" dabbling in theater, I went to many movie-casting calls for Oriental actors. My fantasy was to hit upon a substantial part I could play with dignity. But it was always a madly grinning kamikaze pilot, a no-tickee-no-washee laundryman, a buck-toothed waiter, a coolie railroad worker, or the number-X son of Charlie Chan.

Still there is fun to be had with stereotypes. Take Ito, the Japanese houseboy in *Auntie Mame*, constantly giggling up and down the stairway. I loved auditioning for that cliché role, playing it to the hilt. Although I didn't receive the part, I still find my characterization useful whenever a persistent salesman or a religionist comes to my door to sell me or save me. I go into my act. I giggle hysterically and inform them: "Missy no home. Me Japanese houseboy. No speakee Engrish."

Dependably, they skitter and obsequiously bob their heads backward all the way to their car: "Oh, yes . . . *so sorry* . . . so sorry . . . "

"Sayonara!" I have the rast raugh!

flight
to
the
Moon

山是山

水是水

Mountains

is

Water

Alan Watts was an enthusiastic and conscientious student of Chinese brush calligraphy. For someone starting so late in this art, he used his brush remarkably well.

What I like about his calligraphy is that it expresses transparently all his unique and delightful idiosyncrasies. He has "a lot of character!"

At the height of his celebrated career, he was approached by a number of elite art galleries to exhibit his work. Alan was very flattered and quite excited about the invitations, but he continued to have "cold feet" and managed to find excuses to delay its happening. He confessed to me his trepidation. He asked me to help him to correct some of his obvious calligraphic no-nos.

I had great compassion for his ambivalence, as I was just about to embark on my own fearful journey—trying to write my first book. Alan gave me encouragement and reassurance to trust my style and my simple "talking" prose. I reciprocated by saying to him: "If you try too hard to improve and correct your faults, the best you might achieve would be a relatively fault-free, bland, and uninteresting hand."

Would we prefer to show a middling imitation or an original one-of-a-kind interpretation with a foreign accent?

We chose to honor the latter.

KAI   MEN   JIEN   SHAN

"Open the Gate to See the Mountain."

This is a popular everyday expression meaning "Express yourself openly and clearly." It is also a simple Tai Ji exercise to clear one's vision—to sweep the cobwebs from our "attic" and the clutter from our desktops. It is a functional windshield wiper in the storm.

KAI   MEN   JIEN   SHAN

Look at the four characters above.
Perhaps you will recall the *gate (Men)* 門 as the "swinging door" from the previous pages.

Can you also visualize *mountain (Shan)* 山 as showing two foothills surrounding the central peak, with the valleys between?

Open (Kai) 開 includes the latch 开 that must be unlocked to open the gate.

The old pictograph of *See (Jien)* looks like this, 見 Can you see the Cyclopean eye upon a man?

If you enjoy deciphering these pictographs, try juxtaposing them for fun.

Perhaps you might arrive at a personal composite—a brand-new score for your everyday useful dance.

Look at this example:

Mountain *within* gate or mountain *beyond* gate?

Brook Sprouts

Music, like Tao, contains all the glory of sound and silence. Ancient Chinese sages played contemplative one-note music to quiet the mind. Today we are challenged by the infinite variety of tonal intricacies and contrapuntal sonority.

When I first saw a symphonic score I was bewildered. What remarkable feat could transform such a complexity into cohesive sound? For a long time I could not understand the relationship between the separate realities of what I saw and what I heard.

Later, feeling the need to study various scores, moving slowly through webs of sound and feelings, I found an amicable connection: I looked at the individual notes as musical sprouts growing from the many-layered Earth-lines of the musical score. Different composers have different gardens, arranging their plants with delightful variety and individuality.

I had made my breakthrough! I began to comprehend Western music. I gained easy access to many new friends through their "gardens."

One very special friend came into my life—Johann Sebastian Bach. It was instant love. He became my hero, my teacher, my companion, my playmate—forever! I have found in Bach a divine gardener whose dancing sprouts, for all their profusion, never seem to get in one another's way. Each is fully realized. His flowers bloom all seasons in perfect order and glorious harmony.

Bach is like his name—in English, "brook." The Tao. The watercourse way.

His original manuscripts are calligraphically breath-taking. They are music for both the eyes and the senses— waves of dancing energy. When I dance to Bach, I dance *with* Bach as well. I hang his flowing scores all around the walls of my studio. I am amidst them. He is in me. My body sprouts Bach's music, moving us both in the watercourse way, through time and space.

I took a Japanese Buddhist friend, visiting the United States for the first time, to hear some jazz. His comment: "How very Zen!"

Zen? The smoke-filled nightclub?

Yet nothing could be more Zen than Louis Armstrong's definition of jazz: "If you gotta ask, you'll never know."

We often play and dance to jazz in my Tai Ji sessions. I have found it is wonderful for defrosting the icicle-joints of my students. It sets their heads and bodies moving, often to their surprise.

I think it is significant that one doesn't *define* jazz—one *digs* it. That very physical word speaks of immediacy. And immediacy is the essence of Zen, too, experienced here-now without the delay of thought and definition. Dancing to jazz, you are *getting down, digging, grooving* right now—not just thinking about it.

The Tao of both jazz and zen is to be *with it* or you've lost it. It's gone!

One of the great "jazzzen" masters was D. T. Suzuki, the primary catalyst for introducing Zen to the Western mind. He was getting on in years, and whispers were circulating that he might be dozing off during conferences. At one such meeting he sat, eyes closed, nodding slightly. Someone nearby opened a window and the sudden draft sent papers on the table swirling. With a swiftness to match the wind, Dr. Suzuki reached out, caught the papers on the fly before anyone else could respond, and then promptly returned to his repose.

As the story of this incident spread, "doing a Suzuki" became a phrase to describe the quality of being totally with the moment (whatever the outward appearance).

And that reminds me of a "flip-side" dozing story about another Zen great—the late Alan Watts. Alan and I were part of a panel at a large conference. Alan had been traveling, and he arrived tired and late the previous day. He had stayed up even later enjoying conversation and the grape. The next morning we sat in a crowded, stuffy conference room, listening to the talk drone on.

From the audience Alan might have looked quite alert, but I could see from the corner of my eye that he was sound asleep. A man in the audience was directing to Alan one of those long, involved philosophical question-monologues. Finally he finished and stood there expectantly.

The silence stretched. I began to wonder how I could unobtrusively nudge Alan, or "Ahem" loudly. After what seemed an eternity I noticed his eyes flutter and slowly open. He must have felt the weight of the entire room focused on him. Absolutely unflustered, he solemnly nodded his head and uttered one word: *"Yes."*

"Oh, thank you, thank you!" gushed the man in the audience, obviously grateful for the long and thoughtful consideration his question had been given by no less than Alan Watts.

Dance
with
Papa

My father never changed my diaper, read me a nursery rhyme, tucked me in bed, helped me use building blocks, or ever flew a kite with me. He was a typical old-fashioned Chinese father, an important man, proper and correct in his own way.

He never cooked, washed, or did any household chores. He wouldn't have known how to shop for food or clothing. We had servants and chauffeurs. He had only to ring for everything he needed.

He never took the garbage out!

I love my father. But I am sorry he missed all the fun of our growing up. I am more fortunate than he to be a whole parent. I wish I could offer him some of my own joys and riches.

I miss him!

Father was a gregarious man. He loved people of all types, ages, and professions. He invited every visitor to stay for meals. From time to time he had as many as twenty-five last-minute guests.

Our cooks went crazy with budgeting and planning. They complained to my mother constantly and quit one after another.

Many visitors clearly took advantage of Father's generosity, using our house as a free-meal stop. As children, we thought father was a number-one sucker. But he knew very well what he was doing. He was enjoying his position as the hub of the wheel. The world flocked to him, and he engaged it in stimulating conversation, became its counselor and a most willing listener to everyone in need of reflection.

When he died, hundreds came to pay homage and lament the loss of a bountiful host—one who set his "round tables" with *food* for *thought* as well as for the belly.

I had been in America eleven years before I could find an opportunity to revisit my father. I had concealed from him my career as a dancer-educator because I knew that in writing I couldn't successfully explain to him why my architecture degree put me on the stage instead of behind the drafting table.

Then Suzanne and I received a Ford Foundation grant to return to Taiwan for a year of exploration in the synthesis of East-West Theatre/Dance. My father was shocked at this revelation, but he earnestly tried to understand and support us.

At the end of a year of teaching Taiwan's most promising dancers, we celebrated our results in two major concerts at the City Hall Auditorium. Before the tickets went on sale, I discovered with great frustration that Father had taken the liberty to block a major portion of the best seats for all his important government and social friends, few of whom had any interest in dance whatsoever. I was furious with him! Those VIPs ought to support the arts and *me* by paying for the tickets. No freebies!

Father thought I was too "modern" and insensitive to the old ways and that I ought to have more respect for elders. I should consider it an honor and duty to have the dignitaries' participation. We were at odds and found no immediate resolution.

Unfortunately, the press got wind of this. Realizing the timeliness of this heated controversy, they ran editorials exploring "East *vs.* West," "Tradition *vs.* Modernity," "Arts *vs.* Filial Piety" for a whole week.

The ticket sales soared. The concerts were sold out, with black-market scalpers' prices doubling and tripling. We were a huge artistic and popular success.

Father deemed himself an overnight expert on the modern dance. He became a prodigious and conscientious entrepreneur for his son's new, "honorable" career.

Lin Yutang was one of the first "Quantum Soup" gourmets. His classic, *The Importance of Living*, was equally enlightening in the West and back home in China. He has been my hero since childhood.

I eventually had the privilege of meeting him. My father had arranged to take me to his home one afternoon.

While having tea, Lin said to me, reinforcing his well-known philosophy: "It takes a lot of courage for a person to declare, with clarity and simplicity, that the purpose of life is to *enjoy* it! If you enjoy your dancing and live your dancing, then the purpose of life *is* the *dance*. Congratulations!"

I shall never forget my father's beaming face!

When the news came that I was to be awarded Taiwan's Gold Medal for Outstanding Achievement in the Arts by the Ministry of Culture, I visualized my father's pomposity among his VIP peers.

The award ceremony was to be televised nationwide. On that day my wife and I drove to Father's house, fully expecting him to be all spruced up in his uniform and medals, ready to go with us to the gala affair. But we found him still in his dressing gown and slippers. He explained: "Minister Yen was once a student of mine. If I accompany you there, he will be obliged to say to me, 'General Huang, you have a remarkable son.' Go by yourself. I wish him to say to you, 'Mr. Huang, you are a wonderful artist!'"

Suzanne and I stood transfixed. We had underestimated him. He had been dancing all along!

An Empty Cup of Soup

A classic Zen story tells of a pompous intellect who goes to a Zen master to ask about Zen. The master suggests they have tea. He pours tea into his visitor's cup until it spills over the brim, and yet he continues to pour. Finally, the visitor blurts out: "But my cup is full; it will hold no more!"

"Exactly," says the master, "and like your cup, your mind is full of your own beliefs and ideas. I can give you nothing until you first empty your cup."

I am reminded of this story when folks come to my seminars apparently more intent on showing what they already know than in learning something new. What is puzzling is that they often come back time and again, their cups still full of their own particular soup—so brimful that they cannot accept even a dash of salt and pepper.

I have various ways of inducing my students to empty their cups and be more receptive to learning. At first, they wish to hold on to their acquired "knowledge," not about to leave it at the door. I assure them that they can pick up their "precious" old knowledge on the way out (if they still want it) on the same hanger with their hats and coats or in the pile where their shoes are. They do have a choice to wish to be open.

A few students cling so long to their full cups that I sometimes wish to retaliate by teaching like the old masters in China—with iron discipline and demand for obeisance. No one kept a full cup with them long—the master would smack it out of your hand! It was customary to kowtow to such masters, dropping to touch your forehead to the ground.

One particular person especially brought out this fantasy in me. Haughtily, he would show off what he already knew, yet he faded into the background whenever some new learning threatened him, often slipping out for a nicotine fix. After a few days, I accepted that there was little hope of changing his receptivity. His cup had a *lid* on it.

On the last afternoon of the workshop he stopped me to demonstrate how he did a particular Tai Ji phrase. He was extremely pleased with himself. He had a superficial facility, and I complimented him on his form. Then he asked me if I would like to learn something from *him*. I smiled, wondering how empty *my* cup was in this situation. "Well," he said, "I happen to be a highly skillful group leader myself, and this morning you were *quite bad!*"

I dropped to the floor and kowtowed to him.

One Pinch Less

My wife, Suzanne, is a trained dancer. During her conservatory days, her ballet instructor gave the students the image of "pinching a dime" to firm up their buttocks. (I leave it to your imagination to work out the details.)

I think maybe half of our population took classes with that teacher! Just look around you—the breath-holding expressions and the uptight pinching-dime way of moving.

Don't you wonder what all that *holding on* is *holding in?*

In my classes, I tell everyone the pinching story and then suggest that they all "drop their dimes." The physical release helps liberate the psyche. Many of the self-inflicted repressions just drop away with the dime. Breathing seems easier. Movement becomes more fluid.

Maybe pinching your dime is appropriate when you practice ballet's cross-legged fifth position, but you cannot do Tai Ji that way. Or make love. Or dance freely.

If you are pinching your dime, either physically or psychically, take a risk. Let it go.

Dimes away!

127

Rehearse the Embrace of the Hearse Tiger

My first book takes its title from the most potent metaphor in Tai Ji practice—*Embrace Tiger, Return to Mountain*. The meaning is manifold. *Embrace* implies accepting and welcoming—not clutching. *Tiger* is the dragon, the bull in universal myths of heroic encounters. We face the beast (or angel), befriend it, conquer it, and become one with it.

A frequently used Chinese four-character idiom, *Chi Who Nan Sha*, means word by word, "Ride Tiger Difficult Getoff," or getting stuck with an obligation or challenge.

What if that challenge is *life* itself? Why would you want to get off? Embrace it. Welcome and accept all that life offers. Take it all in and *Return to Mountain*.

128

Return (Gui) traces us to our heritage, our roots. The character shows a person honoring his ancestral tomb, sweeping the gravesite with a broom. *Gui* is to return, to rediscover our origins.

Mountain (Shan) is your home base, not the next "Everest" you must climb! Your mountain is your summit and your bedrock. To return and return again, home.

山

In my teacher-training workshops, we take turns being teacher and student. A french woman was asked to explore various Tai Ji metaphors in front of the class. Her Gallic English was refreshing and often innovative.

While guiding us through a movement motif, *Mounting the Mystical Horse*, she cheerily shouted out, "Now . . . embrace the *hearse!*"

To embrace the "hearse" is one of our ultimate human gestures. Each of us will die someday. Learning to die is not an easy task, particularly in a culture where we constantly avoid the issue until we have to face it. We find ourselves totally unprepared for it.

In most of my seminars, the age group ranges from twenty to eighty. For the youthful ones, to speak of "death and rebirth" is merely a day-to-day metaphor. But to those who have parents and loved ones who are dead or dying, and to those who are themselves in their autumn-winter years, it becomes a different matter.

In Tai Ji movement, the recurring theme of *Embrace Tiger, Return to Mountain* prepares us to embrace our own strength, our weaknesses, our joys, and our sorrows . . . our life-force and our eventual "hearse-tiger" as well.

Every time we practice this dancing round, we re-hearse for the mounting of the metaphoric horse-hearse and enjoy the merry-go-round of this eternal cycle.

130

Returns 歸 Sweeping the Ancestral Tomb

Paradox

In a popular Broadway musical, the Caliph prince walks in an enchanted garden, encountering a beauty. He implores her to take his hand, singing that he is lost in a wonderland and a stranger in paradise. These days, the fate (*kismet*) of our paradise is in question. And like desert sand, the paradigm is definitely shifting. So we find ourselves awobble in *paradox*—spinning with yes/no, up/down, left/right, true/false, confused by an agony of choices that appear to be contradictory. We are strangers in paradox, unsettled and fidgety, in a wonderland of seemingly exclusive possibilities.

And with no hand to take.

Perhaps we need to look at paradox in a new way—more naively and accepting—recognizing the reasonableness of accepting yes/no, at the same time finding a new logic in the illogical, a new consistency in the inconsistent, and embracing absurdity as making quite good, if different, sense.

Albert Einstein said he did not believe that "God plays dice with the universe," and so he remained uncomfortable with the new quantum theory when it came along, a theory that abounds with chance, randomness, and paradox. Yet now we have a whole new generation of physicists who are quite at ease with paradox. In fact, they encourage us to take *their* hand, let go of old patterns and open the way to new worlds for ourselves and for our children. They ask us to leave behind the world of either/or for the world of both/and. Paradox is part and parcel of the new physics.

Perhaps the new Garden of Eden looks like a futuristic Disneyland where God and angels play Go and offer us sugar Rubik Cubes for our tea. Maurits Escher designs the stairways, and we play antique video games with R2D2. Extraterrestrials are come-and-go guests, friends to all, conversing in metaphors. Bread-and-butterflies hover over all.

So many hands! Strangers no more.

132

and Cream Cheese on Dry

Thinkers

Soft & Hard Boiled

Remember as schoolchildren, when we were caught daydreaming, we would quickly add a "thinking hard" grimace? If we seemed to be showing an effort, it somehow made everything okay. Anything that came easy—like daydreaming—couldn't qualify as thinking. Concentrating *had* to be dismal, so we made a painful face.

Look at Rodin's *The Thinker*. Ever since I was a child I have had to suppress a personal vision of a man straining on his potty! I know that popping muscles and bulging veins don't always guarantee success in either thinking or in that daily ritual. I have met so many congested "thinkers" and as many unsuccessful "strainers" that I feel the time for revelation is here.

Contrast Rodin's *Thinker* with the contemplating Buddha. Do you see any sign of strain in the "awakened" one? That, just as easily as Rodin's statute, could be a model of either letting thoughts come—or letting wastes go. Both are natural functions, like breathing. Allow them to happen.

Oddly, in the modern world we get so removed from our natural state that we have to read books and take courses in how to do natural things—make love, give birth, dance . . . .

Flip over this obsession for lesson taking to see how silly it can become. Go outside and give lessons to nature. Explain to the grass how to grow. Shout at the leaves to change color in the fall. Entreat the flowers to bloom in the spring. Require all birds to pass FAA license tests and give fish Red Cross certificates.

Wait a minute. One last lesson. Sit quietly and contemplate nature. Learn about nonstraining.

静坐

Sitting Quietly
Doing Nothing

In Zen archery, when you shoot the arrow from the bow, your *hara-tant'ien* collects all the energy generated from the practice. The discipline is to focus on the bull's-eye—not the obvious one in the target but your own bull's-eye in the physical-psychic center of your gut.

Mystically, the arrow you let fly from the bow needs to make a complete circle through the target and back to your center, like a boomerang returning home. The true marksman keeps his eye on his own center.

One afternoon at a month-long conference on Buddhism and the Mind, a Japanese master demonstrated to us the art of Zen archery. He knelt by a picturesque rock near the edge of the sea. After a long period of meditation with about one hundred of us quietly observing, he stood up and drew an arrow from the quiver around his bare shoulder. He began aiming— out over the open sea!

Aha! He let out a thunderous shout when the arrow flew out of his bow. His small body, glowing with vibrancy, was suddenly a rainbow-colored giant, magnificent to behold!

As I slowly recovered from goose bumps, I realized

of Bull

that many of the onlookers, unfortunately, had missed the main event. Their eyes had followed the arrow to the sea and had bypassed the *real* bull's-eye—the person.

We must recognize fully that the real target is within ourselves—not *out there*.

"Making it" in the world seems to be something *out there*. Yet without the inward satisfaction, the inner awareness, you have missed the target. It must strike home.

You are the target!

One of my favorite cosmic jokes: All his life a man struggles to reach the top of the ladder, and, finally, he does—only to discover it's against the wrong wall!

And another, slightly yellow-humored: A tormented samurai prepares to commit the act of hara-kiri (literally "cutting out one's gut") to salvage some nobility in his life. With great fanfare he takes the dagger, aims for his hara—and misses. *Oops!*

Before you scatter your arrows everywhere—fruitlessly searching, reaching to distant horizons, chasing fleeting rainbows—find your own *center*. Aim at yourself.

Out there is really *in here!*

A Wink of Tao?!

One of the many translations of Tai Ji is the "Great Ultimate," or the "Ultimate Reality."

After I had conducted a Taoism seminar in Santa Cruz, a young man clutching a tape recorder and wearing knitted eyebrows came up to me, "It said in the catalogue, about your seminar, that you would explain the Ultimate Reality. Did you talk about it, or did I miss it?"

Portrait of the Absolute

IN APPRECIATION OF F.C.S. SCHILLER, OXFORD PRAGMATIST
(1864-1937)

乾杯

Bottoms up!

To all my teachers and good friends who have helped me to grow along my way.